The Barbecue

written by Jeremy Strong
illustrated by Jan Smith

Chapter One
Exciting News

Donut whispered to Jojo. "We're going to have a party next weekend. Everybody is coming."
Jojo grinned. "I bet Father Christmas won't be there."
"He will," said Donut. "And Mother Christmas too."
"You're mad!"
Donut pulled a silly face.

Mrs Ambrose saw him. "If you pull a face like that, when the wind changes direction, you'll have a silly face forever!"

"My stepdad says that is why his nose is bent to one side," said Donut.

Everyone laughed.

"You're a clown," smiled Mrs Ambrose. "Now, get on with your work."

Donut leaned across the table again.
"Mum is going to be forty, so we're throwing a party. You and Mouse are invited, and Ben and Sam and Billy and Ravi and and … the whole world!"

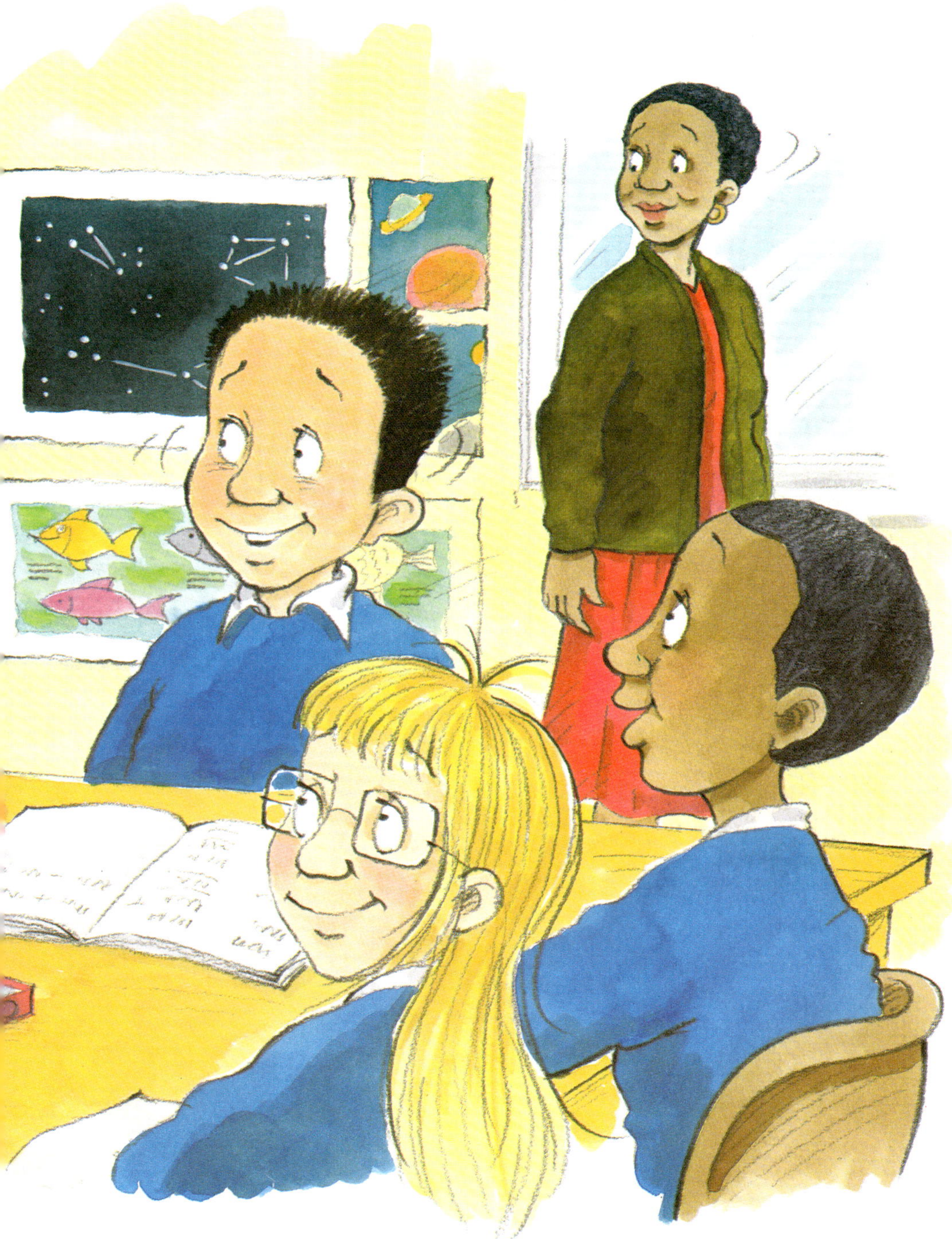

Sam was thinking. Her Dad would be working, so he couldn't go, and that would upset Mum. Sam's mum and dad hardly ever did anything together any more.

"Cheer up, Sam!" cried Donut. "It's a party!"

Sam smiled, but she was sad inside.

"It's going to be really good," Donut went on.
"We're having a barbecue. The last time we had
a barbecue my stepdad set fire to the garden fence.
Mum had to call out the fire brigade."
"You're making that up," said Jojo.
"I'm not!"

At playtime Donut told all his friends about the barbecued fence.

"He's making it up," insisted Jojo.

Donut found his little sister, Cleo, and they all stood round her.

"Cleo, tell everyone what happened last time we had a barbecue."

"We ate sausages," she said, and everyone laughed.
"And then what happened?" said Sam.

Cleo looked at them. "Uncle David's dog threw up," she said.

"CLEO! WHAT HAPPENED TO THE FENCE?"

"It caught fire and the firefighters came and put it out."

Donut smiled at last. "There. Now do you believe me?"

Sam asked Cleo if Uncle David's dog was all right now.

"No," said Cleo. "He's dead."

"Oh dear," said Sam, turning pale. She whispered to Donut. "Did your mum's barbecue cooking kill the dog?"

Donut rolled his eyes. "Of course not! The dog died months later. He died in his sleep, of old age. Cleo, stop making things difficult for me. Go and play with your friends."

But Cleo wanted to play with Sam.
"I'll be a dog and I'm dying. You can be the vet and you save me."
"Brilliant!" smiled Sam. "Come on."
Donut scowled at Cleo. "I'd have her put down," he muttered.

Chapter Two
The Singing Tree

Barbecue day arrived and everyone brought presents for Cassandra Pringle, because it was her birthday.

"Beautiful flowers! Thank you. Oh, a bottle of bubbly. Lubbly bubbly! Thank you."

Mr and Mrs King had brought Big G and Little G with them. "I have brought you a bottle of my homemade barbecue sauce," Big G told Mr Pringle. "Put it on the chicken legs. It will blow their socks off."

"Give us a kiss!" cried Icarus, and Big G burst out laughing.

"That parrot is such a clown," he said.

The children went round carrying trays with nibbles and drinks.

"I bet my mum starts dancing," said Ben with a grin. "She always dances at parties."

Tessa nodded. "She's brilliant. I wish I could dance like Mum."

"It will be okay if your mum dances," said Donut, "but my stepdad nearly always sings at parties. You don't want to hear that!"

But Colin Pringle was too busy cooking. His wife slipped an arm round his waist.

"Darling, this is such a lovely party. Are you sure the fire is not too close to the fence?"

"The fire is fine," said Mr Pringle.

"Watch the fence!"

At last the food
was ready.
"It looks really tasty,"
said Sam's mum.
Mr Pringle smiled.
"Where's your
husband, Jill?"

The plate dropped from Mrs Summerday's
hands and Stinker gobbled up the spilled food.
Sam quickly gave her mum
a clean plate.
"Dad's working,"
Sam said, almost in
a whisper, and they
moved on.

17

Cassandra Pringle went round filling everyone's glass. They sang *Happy Birthday* to her and she cried. "I am so happy," she kept blubbing. "Now I will play for all my friends. Colin, darling, help give a push with the piano."

"Oh no," groaned Donut. "Mum's going to play the piano. That means my stepdad will start singing."

Cassandra sat down and began to play. She was very, very good. Colin Pringle went and stood next to his wife. He began to sing. He was very, very bad.

Mr Pringle sang **louder** and **louder**.

Then he began to climb the big oak tree.

He clung to the topmost branches and sang like a giant bird.
"That is the worst singing I've ever heard," giggled Trish Macdonald.

Cassandra stopped playing the piano.
She shouted up to her husband. "Colin, stop singing. Come down here at once, you silly man!"
"I can't," said Mr Pringle. "I'm stuck."

Ben's parents burst out laughing, and soon everyone was rolling about. But Cassandra Pringle was very angry.

"You stupid, big budgerigar!" she shouted.
"I can't get down!" squawked Mr Pringle. "Someone help me, please. I don't want to die up here!"

Chapter Three
Sam's Dad to the Rescue

"We must call the fire brigade," suggested Mr Gohill.

"No! We had to call out the firefighters last time!" said Mrs Pringle, but Mr Gohill rang the fire brigade and asked if they could help.

A fire engine came screeching to a halt outside the house. Sam's dad jumped out. Sam ran across to see him.

"Donut's stepdad is stuck up a tree," Sam told her dad.

Mr Summerday looked in the back garden. "Don't worry, Mr Pringle. We shall soon have you back on the ground."

"Oh, my darling Colin! If something happens to him I'll die. Please be careful!" sniffed Mrs Pringle.
Sam's father climbed into the lift cage.
Sam watched proudly. "My dad's going to save your dad."

The lift went up and Sam's dad helped Mr Pringle climb into the cage. They came back down to the garden safely.

Cassandra Pringle flew at her husband. "Are you all right?" she cried, kissing his face. Then she flew into a rage. "You mad baboon! What am I going to do with you?" Cassandra began kissing her husband again.

Sam watched them both and wondered why her parents could not be like the Pringles.

Mr Pringle gazed sheepishly at the grinning firefighters.

"Would you like to join us for a barbecue?" he asked. So they did, and it was brilliant. They finished with dancing. Tessa was quite right. Mrs King was the best dancer of all. But who did Donut dance with?

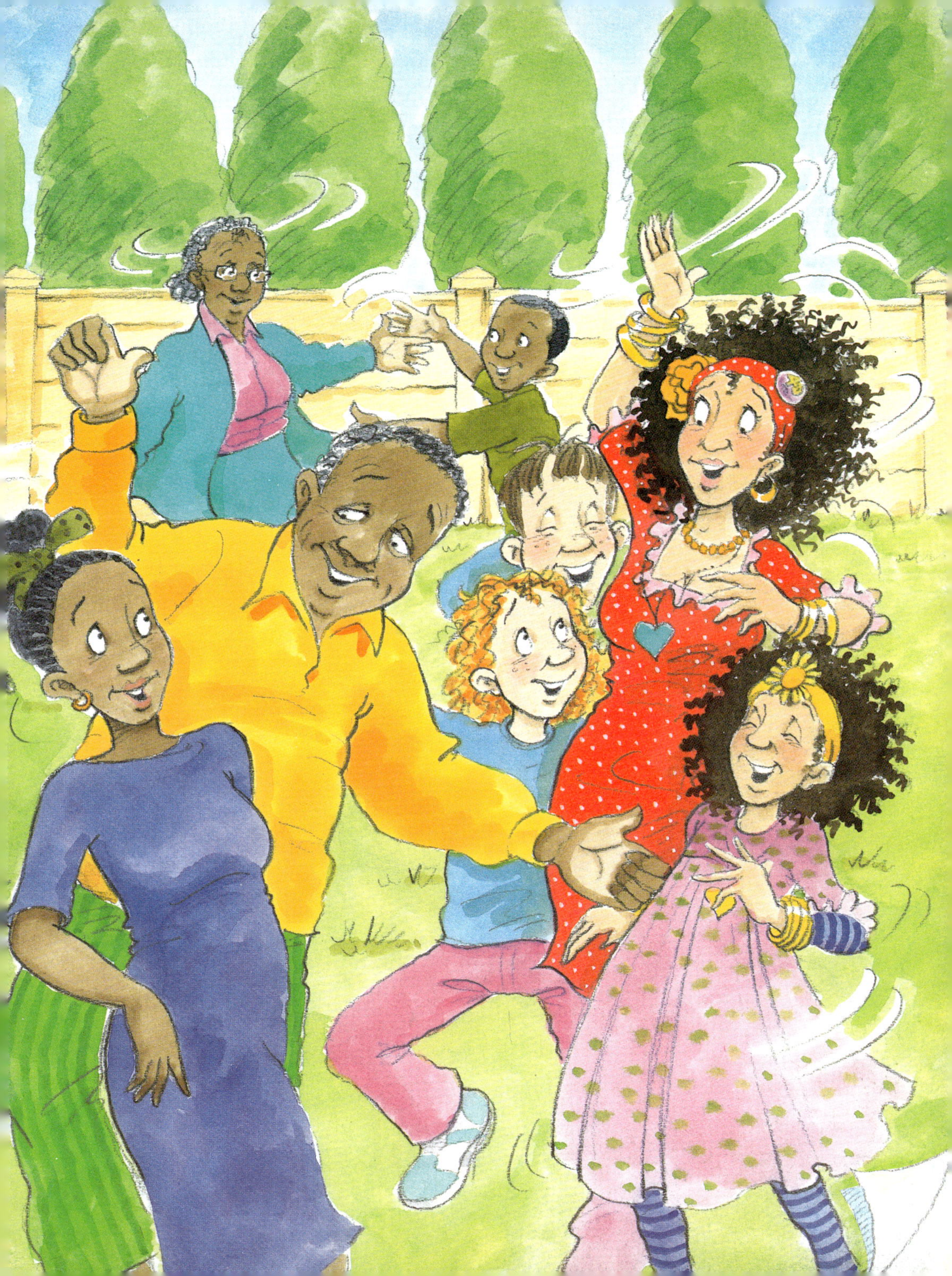

Mrs Ambrose!